Gourmet Grape Jam

A Cookbook Celebrating the Versatility of Grapes

GOURMET GRAPE JAM

First edition. February 17, 2024.

ISBN: 979-8224441310

Written by Jose Maria.

Table of Contents

Jose Maria

❖ Introduction to Grape Jam

Grape jam holds a special place in culinary history, boasting a rich heritage and significance that stretches back centuries. From ancient civilizations to modern-day kitchens, grape jam has remained a beloved condiment cherished for its sweet, tangy flavor and versatile applications.

A. History and Significance of Grape Jam

Grape jam traces its roots back to ancient times, with evidence of grape preservation methods dating back to civilizations such as the Mesopotamians, Egyptians, and Greeks. These ancient cultures recognized the value of grapes not only as a delicious fruit but also for their potential to be transformed into long-lasting preserves.

Throughout history, grape jam has been prized for its ability to preserve the harvest, providing sustenance during lean times and adding sweetness to meals year-round. In medieval Europe, grape jam became a staple in noble households and monasteries, where it was often paired with bread, cheese, and meats.

The popularity of grape jam continued to grow over the centuries, spreading to regions around the world as trade routes expanded and culinary traditions evolved. Today, grape jam remains a beloved pantry staple enjoyed by people of all ages and cultures.

B. Varieties of Grapes Used in Jam Making

Grapes come in a diverse array of varieties, each with its own unique flavor profile, color, and texture. When it comes to making grape jam, the choice of grape can significantly impact the taste and character of the final product.

Some of the most commonly used grape varieties for jam making include:

- Concord Grapes: Known for their bold, sweet flavor and distinctive purple hue, Concord grapes are a popular choice for classic grape jam.

- Muscat Grapes: Muscat grapes are prized for their aromatic sweetness, making them an excellent choice for fragrant grape jams.
- Thompson Seedless Grapes: These green grapes are prized for their mild, sweet flavor and are often used to make seedless grape jam.
- Red Globe Grapes: With their vibrant red color and juicy flesh, Red Globe grapes add a beautiful hue and flavor to grape jam recipes.

C. Benefits of Making Homemade Grape Jam

Making homemade grape jam offers a multitude of benefits, including:

1. Quality Control: When making grape jam at home, you have full control over the ingredients used, allowing you to avoid artificial preservatives and additives.
2. Customization: Homemade grape jam recipes can be tailored to suit your taste preferences, whether you prefer a classic sweet jam or a spiced variation with a hint of warmth.
3. Freshness: Homemade grape jam captures the essence of ripe, freshly harvested grapes, ensuring a burst of flavor in every spoonful.
4. Sustainability: Making grape jam at home is a great way to reduce food waste by preserving excess fruit from your garden or local farmers' market.
5. Creative Expression: Experimenting with different grape varieties, flavorings, and spices allows you to unleash your creativity in the kitchen, resulting in unique and delicious jam creations.

By exploring the world of homemade grape jam, you can embark on a culinary journey steeped in tradition, flavor, and endless possibilities.

Whether enjoyed spread on toast, swirled into desserts, or used as a flavorful ingredient in savory dishes, grape jam is sure to add a touch of sweetness to every meal.

Chapter (1) Getting Started

Before diving into the delightful process of making grape jam, it's essential to gather the necessary tools and ingredients and familiarize yourself with some helpful tips for selecting the best grapes.

A. Essential Tools and Equipment

Large, Heavy-Bottomed Pot: Choose a pot with a thick, heavy bottom to prevent scorching and ensure even cooking of the jam.

1. Canning Jars: Mason jars or other heat-resistant glass jars with lids are ideal for storing homemade grape jam.
2. Canning Funnel: A canning funnel makes filling jars with hot jam much easier and helps prevent spills.
3. Jar Lifter: This tool is essential for safely lifting hot jars in and out of boiling water during the canning process.
4. Ladle: Use a ladle to transfer the hot jam into jars, ensuring even distribution and minimal mess.
5. Jam Thermometer: While not strictly necessary, a jam thermometer can help ensure that your jam reaches the proper setting point for optimal consistency.

B. Ingredients Overview

To make classic grape jam, you'll need:

- Grapes: Choose ripe, flavorful grapes for the best-tasting jam. Concord grapes are traditional, but you can experiment with other varieties for unique flavors.
- Sugar: Granulated sugar acts as a preservative and sweetens the jam. You can adjust the amount of sugar to suit your taste preferences.
- Lemon Juice: Lemon juice adds acidity, which helps the jam set and preserves its vibrant color.

- Pectin (optional): Pectin is a natural thickening agent found in fruits. Adding pectin can help the jam achieve a firmer set in less time.

C. Tips for Selecting the Best Grapes for Jam

When selecting grapes for jam making, keep the following tips in mind:

- Ripe and Flavorful: Choose grapes that are ripe, fragrant, and bursting with flavor. Avoid grapes that are underripe or overly soft.
- Seedless vs. Seeded: Decide whether you prefer seeded or seedless grape jam. Seedless varieties are convenient but may lack the depth of flavor found in seeded grapes.
- Varietal Selection: Experiment with different grape varieties to discover unique flavor profiles. Consider combining multiple grape varieties for complex flavor combinations.
- Organic Options: If possible, opt for organic grapes to minimize exposure to pesticides and other chemicals.

By equipping yourself with the right tools and ingredients and selecting the best grapes for your jam, you'll set yourself up for success in creating delicious homemade grape jam that will delight your taste buds and impress your friends and family.

Chapter (2) Basic Grape Jam Recipes

Grape jam comes in various forms, catering to different preferences and dietary needs. Here are four basic grape jam recipes to suit every taste.

A. Classic Grape Jam

Ingredients:

- 4 cups ripe grapes, stemmed and washed
- 2 cups granulated sugar
- 1 tablespoon lemon juice

Instructions:

1. In a large, heavy-bottomed pot, combine the grapes and sugar. Let the mixture sit for about 30 minutes to allow the sugar to dissolve slightly and the flavors to meld.
2. Place the pot over medium heat and bring the mixture to a boil, stirring occasionally to prevent sticking.
3. Once boiling, reduce the heat to medium-low and simmer the jam, stirring frequently, until it thickens and reaches the desired consistency, about 45-60 minutes. Skim off any foam that rises to the surface.
4. Stir in the lemon juice and continue to cook for an additional 5 minutes.
5. To test if the jam is ready, place a small amount on a chilled plate and run your finger through it. If the jam holds its shape without immediately flowing back together, it's done.
6. Remove the pot from the heat and let the jam cool slightly.
7. Transfer the jam to sterilized jars, leaving about ¼ inch of headspace. Seal the jars tightly with lids.
8. If canning for long-term storage, process the jars in a boiling water bath for 10 minutes. Otherwise, let the jam cool

completely before refrigerating.

B. Seedless Grape Jam
Ingredients:

- 4 cups seedless grapes, washed
- 2 cups granulated sugar
- 1 tablespoon lemon juice

Instructions:

1. Follow the same instructions as for Classic Grape Jam, substituting seedless grapes for seeded grapes.

C. Low-Sugar Grape Jam
Ingredients:

- 4 cups ripe grapes, stemmed and washed
- 1 cup granulated sugar (or sweetener of choice)
- 1 tablespoon lemon juice
- 1 tablespoon low-sugar pectin (optional)

Instructions:

1. In a large, heavy-bottomed pot, combine the grapes and sugar (or sweetener). Let the mixture sit for about 30 minutes.
2. Add the lemon juice and pectin (if using) to the pot and stir well.
3. Place the pot over medium heat and bring the mixture to a boil, stirring occasionally.
4. Reduce the heat to medium-low and simmer the jam, stirring frequently, until it thickens and reaches the desired consistency, about 45-60 minutes.
5. Follow steps 5-8 from the Classic Grape Jam recipe to finish and

store the jam.

D. Spiced Grape Jam
Ingredients:

- 4 cups ripe grapes, stemmed and washed
- 2 cups granulated sugar
- 1 tablespoon lemon juice
- 1 teaspoon ground cinnamon
- ¼ teaspoon ground cloves
- ¼ teaspoon ground nutmeg

Instructions:

1. In a large, heavy-bottomed pot, combine the grapes, sugar, lemon juice, and spices.
2. Let the mixture sit for about 30 minutes to allow the flavors to meld.
3. Place the pot over medium heat and bring the mixture to a boil, stirring occasionally.
4. Reduce the heat to medium-low and simmer the jam, stirring frequently, until it thickens and reaches the desired consistency, about 45-60 minutes.
5. Follow steps 5-8 from the Classic Grape Jam recipe to finish and store the jam.

These basic grape jam recipes offer a range of flavors and options to suit any preference, whether you prefer the classic sweetness of grape jam or enjoy experimenting with different variations and spice combinations. Enjoy spreading these delicious jams on toast, biscuits, or as a delightful addition to your favorite recipes.

Chapter (3) Beyond the Spread: Creative Grape Jam Applications

Grape jam's versatility extends far beyond the breakfast table. Explore these creative and delicious ways to incorporate grape jam into your culinary repertoire.

A. Grape Jam Thumbprint Cookies
Ingredients:

- 1 cup all-purpose flour
- ½ cup unsalted butter, softened
- ⅓ cup granulated sugar
- ¼ teaspoon vanilla extract
- Grape jam

Instructions:

1. Preheat your oven to 350°F (175°C) and line a baking sheet with parchment paper.
2. In a mixing bowl, cream together the softened butter, sugar, and vanilla extract until light and fluffy.
3. Gradually add the flour to the butter mixture, mixing until a dough forms.
4. Roll the dough into small balls, about 1 inch in diameter, and place them on the prepared baking sheet.
5. Use your thumb or the back of a spoon to make an indentation in the center of each dough ball.
6. Fill each indentation with a small spoonful of grape jam.
7. Bake the cookies in the preheated oven for 10-12 minutes, or until the edges are lightly golden.
8. Allow the cookies to cool on the baking sheet for a few minutes before transferring them to a wire rack to cool completely.

9. Enjoy these delightful grape jam thumbprint cookies with a glass of milk or your favorite hot beverage.

B. Grape Jam Glazed Pork Tenderloin
Ingredients:

- 1 lb pork tenderloin
- Salt and pepper, to taste
- ½ cup grape jam
- 2 tablespoons balsamic vinegar
- 1 tablespoon Dijon mustard
- 2 cloves garlic, minced
- 1 teaspoon dried thyme

Instructions:

1. Preheat your oven to 375°F (190°C).
2. Season the pork tenderloin with salt and pepper, then place it in a baking dish.
3. In a small bowl, whisk together the grape jam, balsamic vinegar, Dijon mustard, minced garlic, and dried thyme to make the glaze.
4. Pour the glaze over the pork tenderloin, making sure it's evenly coated.
5. Roast the pork tenderloin in the preheated oven for 25-30 minutes, or until it reaches an internal temperature of 145°F (63°C).
6. Remove the pork from the oven and let it rest for a few minutes before slicing.
7. Serve the sliced pork tenderloin with additional glaze spooned over the top.

C. Grape Jam and Brie Grilled Cheese
Ingredients:

- Slices of bread (your choice of bread)
- Butter, softened
- Grape jam
- Brie cheese, sliced

Instructions:

1. Heat a skillet or griddle over medium heat.
2. Butter one side of each slice of bread.
3. Spread grape jam on the unbuttered side of one slice of bread.
4. Place slices of Brie cheese on top of the grape jam.
5. Top with the second slice of bread, buttered side facing out.
6. Place the sandwich in the skillet or griddle and cook until the bread is golden brown and the cheese is melted, flipping halfway through.
7. Once both sides are golden brown and the cheese is melted, remove the sandwich from the skillet or griddle.
8. Let the sandwich cool for a minute before slicing it in half and serving.

D. Grape Jam-Filled Cupcakes
Ingredients:

- Your favorite cupcake batter
- Grape jam
- Frosting of your choice

Instructions:

1. Preheat your oven and prepare your favorite cupcake batter according to the recipe instructions.
2. Line a cupcake tin with paper liners.
3. Fill each cupcake liner halfway with batter.
4. Add a teaspoon of grape jam to the center of each cupcake.

5. Top each cupcake with more batter until the liners are about ¾ full.
6. Bake the cupcakes according to the recipe instructions.
7. Let the cupcakes cool completely before frosting them with your favorite frosting.

These creative grape jam applications add a delightful twist to traditional recipes, infusing them with the sweet and tangy flavor of homemade grape jam. Enjoy exploring these inventive ways to incorporate grape jam into your cooking and baking endeavors.

Chapter (4) International Flavors: Grape Jam Around the World

Grape jam transcends cultural boundaries, finding its way into a variety of traditional dishes from around the globe. Explore these international flavors and discover new ways to enjoy the sweet and tangy essence of grape jam.

A. French Grape Confiture
Ingredients:

- 4 cups ripe grapes, stemmed and washed
- 2 cups granulated sugar
- 1 tablespoon lemon juice
- 1 vanilla bean, split lengthwise

Instructions:

1. In a large, heavy-bottomed pot, combine the grapes, sugar, lemon juice, and vanilla bean.
2. Let the mixture sit for about 30 minutes to allow the flavors to meld.
3. Place the pot over medium heat and bring the mixture to a boil, stirring occasionally.
4. Reduce the heat to medium-low and simmer the jam, stirring frequently, until it thickens and reaches the desired consistency, about 45-60 minutes.
5. Remove the pot from the heat and let the jam cool slightly.
6. Remove the vanilla bean from the jam and discard.
7. Transfer the jam to sterilized jars, leaving about ¼ inch of headspace. Seal the jars tightly with lids.
8. If canning for long-term storage, process the jars in a boiling water bath for 10 minutes. Otherwise, let the jam cool

completely before refrigerating.

9. Enjoy this delightful French grape confiture spread on toast, croissants, or as a filling for pastries.

B. Italian Crostata with Grape Jam
Ingredients:

- 1 ½ cups all-purpose flour
- ½ cup granulated sugar
- 1 teaspoon baking powder
- Pinch of salt
- ½ cup unsalted butter, cold and diced
- 1 egg
- 1 teaspoon vanilla extract
- Grape jam
- Powdered sugar, for dusting

Instructions:

1. Preheat your oven to 350°F (175°C) and grease a tart or pie pan.
2. In a large mixing bowl, combine the flour, sugar, baking powder, and salt.
3. Add the cold diced butter to the flour mixture and use your fingers or a pastry cutter to cut the butter into the flour until the mixture resembles coarse crumbs.
4. In a small bowl, whisk together the egg and vanilla extract.
5. Add the egg mixture to the flour mixture and stir until the dough comes together.
6. Press the dough evenly into the greased tart or pie pan, making sure to cover the bottom and sides.
7. Spread a layer of grape jam over the dough in the tart or pie pan.
8. Bake the crostata in the preheated oven for 25-30 minutes, or until the crust is golden brown.

9. Remove the crostata from the oven and let it cool slightly before dusting with powdered sugar.
10. Serve slices of this delicious Italian crostata with grape jam as a delightful dessert or afternoon treat.

C. Turkish Grape Jam Baklava
Ingredients:

- 1 package of phyllo dough
- 1 cup unsalted butter, melted
- 2 cups finely chopped walnuts or pistachios
- 1 teaspoon ground cinnamon
- 1 cup grape jam
- Syrup (made with sugar, water, and lemon juice)

Instructions:

1. Preheat your oven to 350°F (175°C) and grease a baking dish.
2. Lay a sheet of phyllo dough in the greased baking dish and brush it generously with melted butter.
3. Repeat layering phyllo dough and melted butter until you have about 8-10 layers.
4. In a mixing bowl, combine the chopped nuts and ground cinnamon.
5. Spread a layer of nut mixture over the phyllo dough in the baking dish.
6. Drizzle grape jam evenly over the nut layer.
7. Continue layering phyllo dough, melted butter, nut mixture, and grape jam until you have used all of the ingredients, finishing with a final layer of phyllo dough brushed with melted butter.
8. Use a sharp knife to cut the baklava into diamond or square shapes.

9. Bake the baklava in the preheated oven for 35-40 minutes, or until golden brown and crisp.
10. While the baklava is baking, prepare the syrup by heating sugar, water, and lemon juice in a saucepan until the sugar is dissolved and the mixture is slightly thickened.
11. Once the baklava is done baking, remove it from the oven and immediately pour the syrup over the hot baklava.
12. Let the baklava cool completely before serving. Enjoy this decadent Turkish grape jam baklava as a sweet and indulgent dessert.

D. Indian Grape Jam Chutney
Ingredients:

- 4 cups ripe grapes, stemmed and washed
- 1 cup granulated sugar
- 1 tablespoon lemon juice
- 1 teaspoon cumin seeds
- 1 teaspoon mustard seeds
- ½ teaspoon red chili flakes
- Salt, to taste

Instructions:

1. In a large, heavy-bottomed pot, combine the grapes, sugar, lemon juice, cumin seeds, mustard seeds, red chili flakes, and salt.
2. Let the mixture sit for about 30 minutes to allow the flavors to meld.
3. Place the pot over medium heat and bring the mixture to a boil, stirring occasionally.
4. Reduce the heat to medium-low and simmer the chutney, stirring frequently, until it thickens and reaches the desired

consistency, about 45-60 minutes.

5. Remove the pot from the heat and let the chutney cool slightly.
6. Transfer the chutney to sterilized jars, leaving about ¼ inch of headspace. Seal the jars tightly with lids.
7. If canning for long-term storage, process the jars in a boiling water bath for 10 minutes. Otherwise, let the chutney cool completely before refrigerating.
8. Enjoy this flavorful Indian grape jam chutney as a condiment for curries, rice dishes, or grilled meats.

These international grape jam recipes offer a taste of culinary traditions from around the world, showcasing the diverse ways in which grape jam can be used to create delicious and unique dishes. Experiment with these recipes to discover new flavors and expand your culinary horizons.

Chapter (5) Healthier Alternatives: Sugar-Free and Vegan Grape Jam

Enjoy the sweet and vibrant flavors of grape jam with these healthier alternatives that are free from refined sugar and animal products.

A. Sugar-Free Grape Chia Jam

Ingredients:

- 4 cups ripe grapes, stemmed and washed
- 2-3 tablespoons chia seeds
- 1-2 tablespoons lemon juice (optional, for added acidity)

Instructions:

1. In a saucepan, heat the grapes over medium heat until they start to break down and release their juices, about 5-7 minutes.
2. Mash the grapes with a fork or potato masher to help them break down further.
3. Stir in the chia seeds and continue to cook the mixture over medium-low heat, stirring occasionally, until it thickens to your desired consistency, about 15-20 minutes.
4. If desired, add lemon juice to taste for a touch of acidity.
5. Remove the jam from the heat and let it cool completely.
6. Transfer the jam to sterilized jars and store in the refrigerator for up to two weeks.

B. Vegan Grape Jam with Agar Agar

Ingredients:

- 4 cups ripe grapes, stemmed and washed
- 1 cup water

- 2-3 tablespoons agar agar flakes
- 1-2 tablespoons lemon juice (optional, for added acidity)
- Sweetener of your choice (optional, to taste)

Instructions:

1. In a saucepan, combine the grapes and water. Bring to a boil over medium heat, then reduce the heat and simmer for about 10-15 minutes, until the grapes soften.
2. Mash the grapes with a fork or potato masher to release their juices.
3. Stir in the agar agar flakes and continue to simmer for another 5 minutes, stirring constantly, until the mixture thickens.
4. If desired, add lemon juice and sweetener to taste.
5. Remove the jam from the heat and let it cool slightly.
6. Transfer the jam to sterilized jars and let it cool completely before sealing and storing in the refrigerator for up to two weeks.

C. Paleo-Friendly Grape Jam with Honey
Ingredients:

- 4 cups ripe grapes, stemmed and washed
- 2-3 tablespoons raw honey
- 1-2 tablespoons lemon juice (optional, for added acidity)

Instructions:

1. In a saucepan, heat the grapes over medium heat until they start to break down and release their juices, about 5-7 minutes.
2. Mash the grapes with a fork or potato masher to help them break down further.
3. Stir in the raw honey and continue to cook the mixture over medium-low heat, stirring occasionally, until it thickens to your

desired consistency, about 15-20 minutes.
4. If desired, add lemon juice to taste for a touch of acidity.
5. Remove the jam from the heat and let it cool completely.
6. Transfer the jam to sterilized jars and store in the refrigerator for up to two weeks.

These healthier alternatives to traditional grape jam offer the same delicious flavor and versatility while catering to specific dietary preferences. Whether you're looking to reduce your sugar intake, follow a vegan lifestyle, or adhere to a paleo diet, these recipes are sure to satisfy your cravings for homemade grape jam. Enjoy spreading them on toast, swirling them into yogurt, or using them as a topping for pancakes and waffles.

Chapter (6) Preserving and Storing Grape Jam

Preserving and storing grape jam properly ensures that you can enjoy its delicious flavor for an extended period. Explore these methods for long-term storage and helpful tips for keeping your grape jam fresh.

A. Canning Grape Jam for Long-Term Storage

Materials Needed:

- Sterilized canning jars with lids and bands
- Water bath canner or large pot
- Jar lifter
- Canning funnel
- Clean cloth or paper towels

Instructions:

1. Prepare your grape jam according to your chosen recipe.
2. While the jam is still hot, carefully ladle it into sterilized canning jars, leaving about ¼ inch of headspace at the top.
3. Wipe the rims of the jars with a clean, damp cloth or paper towel to remove any residue.
4. Place the lids and bands on the jars, making sure they are tightened securely.
5. Using a jar lifter, lower the filled jars into a water bath canner or large pot filled with boiling water, making sure the jars are fully submerged and have at least 1-2 inches of water covering the tops.
6. Process the jars in the boiling water bath for the recommended time specified in your recipe, typically around 10-15 minutes.
7. Once processed, carefully remove the jars from the water bath using the jar lifter and place them on a clean towel or rack to

cool completely.

8. As the jars cool, you should hear a "pop" sound, indicating that the lids have sealed properly. Check the seals by pressing down on the center of each lid. If it doesn't flex or make a popping sound, the jar is sealed.

9. Store the sealed jars of grape jam in a cool, dark place, such as a pantry or cupboard, for long-term storage.

B. Freezing Grape Jam
Instructions:

1. Allow your grape jam to cool completely after preparing it.
2. Transfer the jam to freezer-safe containers or jars, leaving some space at the top to allow for expansion during freezing.
3. Seal the containers tightly and label them with the date.
4. Place the containers of grape jam in the freezer, where they can be stored for up to 6-12 months.
5. When ready to use, thaw the jam in the refrigerator overnight or at room temperature for a few hours. Stir the jam before serving to redistribute any separated juices.

C. Tips for Properly Storing Grape Jam

- Use Clean Jars: Always use clean, sterilized jars for storing grape jam to prevent contamination and spoilage.
- Proper Sealing: Ensure that the jars are tightly sealed to prevent air from entering and causing the jam to spoil.
- Cool Completely: Allow the jam to cool completely before sealing and storing to prevent condensation from forming inside the jars.
- Labeling: Label each jar with the date of preparation to keep track of its shelf life.
- Refrigeration: Once opened, store any remaining grape jam in

the refrigerator to maintain freshness. It can typically last for several weeks when refrigerated.

- Check for Spoilage: Before consuming stored grape jam, always check for signs of spoilage, such as mold growth, off odors, or changes in texture or color. If in doubt, discard the jam.

By following these preservation methods and storage tips, you can ensure that your homemade grape jam remains delicious and safe to consume for months to come. Whether you choose to can, freeze, or refrigerate your jam, proper storage practices are essential for maintaining its quality and flavor.

Chapter (7) Troubleshooting Common Grape Jam Issues

Encounter a hiccup while making grape jam? Here are some common issues and solutions to help you troubleshoot and achieve perfect results every time.

A. Preventing Crystallization

- Issue: Crystallization can occur when sugar in the jam forms large, gritty crystals, resulting in a grainy texture.
- Solution:
- Use fresh ingredients: Ensure that your grapes and sugar are fresh and free from impurities, as older or contaminated ingredients can contribute to crystallization.
- Properly dissolve sugar: Make sure to fully dissolve the sugar in the grape mixture before boiling to prevent crystallization. Stirring the mixture frequently during the heating process can help achieve this.
- Avoid stirring excessively: While cooking the jam, avoid stirring too frequently, as this can introduce air into the mixture and promote crystallization. Stir gently and only as needed.
- Add lemon juice: Adding a small amount of lemon juice to the jam can help prevent crystallization by increasing acidity and inhibiting sugar crystallization.

B. Adjusting Consistency

- Issue: Your grape jam may end up too thin or too thick, affecting its texture and spreadability.
- Solution:
- Test for doneness: Use a thermometer or the "wrinkle test" to determine the jam's readiness. The jam should reach a

temperature of about 220°F (104°C) or form a wrinkled skin when a small amount is placed on a chilled plate and pushed with a finger.

- Adjust cooking time: If the jam is too thin, continue cooking it over low heat until it thickens to the desired consistency. Conversely, if the jam is too thick, you can add a small amount of water or fruit juice to thin it out.

- Use pectin: Adding commercial pectin can help achieve a firmer set and improve the consistency of the jam. Follow the manufacturer's instructions for the appropriate amount to use.

C. Dealing with Mold

- Issue: Mold growth can occur on the surface of grape jam, especially if not properly sealed or stored.
- Solution:
- Proper sealing: Ensure that the jars are tightly sealed after filling and processing to prevent air and moisture from entering, which can promote mold growth.
- Store correctly: Store sealed jars of grape jam in a cool, dark place, such as a pantry or cupboard, to inhibit mold growth. Avoid storing jam in areas with high humidity or temperature fluctuations.
- Refrigerate after opening: Once opened, store any remaining grape jam in the refrigerator to extend its shelf life and prevent mold growth. Always use clean utensils to avoid introducing contaminants.
- Discard if moldy: If you notice any signs of mold growth, such as fuzzy spots or unusual odors, discard the affected jam immediately. Mold can produce harmful toxins that may cause illness if consumed.

By addressing these common issues and following these troubleshooting tips, you can overcome challenges and ensure that your grape jam turns out perfectly every time. With a little attention to detail and proper technique, you'll be enjoying delicious homemade grape jam without any hiccups.

Chapter (8) Exotic Grape Varieties: Exploring Unique Flavors

Discover the distinctive flavors of exotic grape varieties with these delicious jam recipes featuring Concord, Muscadine, Champagne, and Red Globe grapes.

A. Concord Grape Jam

Ingredients:

- 4 cups Concord grapes, stemmed and washed
- 2 cups granulated sugar
- 1 tablespoon lemon juice

Instructions:

1. In a large, heavy-bottomed pot, combine the Concord grapes and sugar. Let the mixture sit for about 30 minutes to allow the sugar to dissolve slightly and the flavors to meld.
2. Place the pot over medium heat and bring the mixture to a boil, stirring occasionally to prevent sticking.
3. Once boiling, reduce the heat to medium-low and simmer the jam, stirring frequently, until it thickens and reaches the desired consistency, about 45-60 minutes. Skim off any foam that rises to the surface.
4. Stir in the lemon juice and continue to cook for an additional 5 minutes.
5. To test if the jam is ready, place a small amount on a chilled plate and run your finger through it. If the jam holds its shape without immediately flowing back together, it's done.
6. Remove the pot from the heat and let the jam cool slightly.
7. Transfer the jam to sterilized jars, leaving about ¼ inch of headspace. Seal the jars tightly with lids.

8. If canning for long-term storage, process the jars in a boiling water bath for 10 minutes. Otherwise, let the jam cool completely before refrigerating.

B. Muscadine Grape Jam
Ingredients:

- 4 cups Muscadine grapes, stemmed and washed
- 2 cups granulated sugar
- 1 tablespoon lemon juice

Instructions:

1. Follow the same instructions as for Concord Grape Jam, substituting Muscadine grapes for Concord grapes.

C. Champagne Grape Jam
Ingredients:

- 4 cups Champagne grapes, stemmed and washed
- 2 cups granulated sugar
- 1 tablespoon lemon juice

Instructions:

1. Follow the same instructions as for Concord Grape Jam, substituting Champagne grapes for Concord grapes.

D. Red Globe Grape Jam
Ingredients:

- 4 cups Red Globe grapes, stemmed and washed
- 2 cups granulated sugar

- 1 tablespoon lemon juice

Instructions:

1. Follow the same instructions as for Concord Grape Jam, substituting Red Globe grapes for Concord grapes.

These exotic grape varieties bring unique flavors and characteristics to your homemade jam, allowing you to explore new taste sensations and culinary experiences. Enjoy these delightful jams spread on toast, biscuits, or incorporated into your favorite recipes for a touch of exotic flair.

Chapter (9) Holiday Grape Jam Creations

Celebrate the festive spirit with these holiday-inspired grape jam creations, perfect for Thanksgiving, Christmas, and Easter gatherings.

A. Thanksgiving Cranberry-Grape Jam
Ingredients:

- 2 cups cranberries, fresh or frozen
- 2 cups seedless red grapes
- 1 ½ cups granulated sugar
- 1 tablespoon orange zest
- 1 tablespoon lemon juice
- ½ teaspoon ground cinnamon
- Pinch of ground cloves
- Pinch of salt

Instructions:

1. In a saucepan, combine the cranberries, grapes, sugar, orange zest, lemon juice, cinnamon, cloves, and salt.
2. Cook over medium heat, stirring occasionally, until the fruits soften and release their juices, about 10-15 minutes.
3. Mash the fruits with a potato masher or fork to break them down further.
4. Continue to cook the mixture, stirring frequently, until it thickens to a jam-like consistency, about 15-20 minutes.
5. Remove the jam from the heat and let it cool slightly.
6. Transfer the jam to sterilized jars and let it cool completely before sealing.
7. Store the jars in the refrigerator for up to two weeks or follow the canning process for long-term storage.

B. Christmas Spiced Grape Jam

Ingredients:

- 4 cups seedless black grapes
- 2 cups granulated sugar
- 1 tablespoon lemon juice
- 1 teaspoon ground cinnamon
- ½ teaspoon ground nutmeg
- ½ teaspoon ground cloves
- Pinch of salt

Instructions:

1. In a large saucepan, combine the grapes, sugar, lemon juice, cinnamon, nutmeg, cloves, and salt.
2. Cook over medium heat, stirring occasionally, until the grapes soften and release their juices, about 10-15 minutes.
3. Mash the grapes with a potato masher or fork to break them down further.
4. Continue to cook the mixture, stirring frequently, until it thickens to a jam-like consistency, about 15-20 minutes.
5. Remove the jam from the heat and let it cool slightly.
6. Transfer the jam to sterilized jars and let it cool completely before sealing.
7. Store the jars in the refrigerator for up to two weeks or follow the canning process for long-term storage.

C. Easter Grape Jam Tart
Ingredients:

- 1 pre-made pie crust or homemade pastry dough
- 2 cups seedless green grapes
- ½ cup granulated sugar
- 2 tablespoons cornstarch
- 1 tablespoon lemon juice
- 1 teaspoon vanilla extract
- Egg wash (1 egg beaten with 1 tablespoon water)
- Powdered sugar, for dusting

Instructions:

1. Preheat your oven to 375°F (190°C) and prepare a tart pan or pie dish with the pie crust or pastry dough.
2. In a saucepan, combine the green grapes, sugar, cornstarch, lemon juice, and vanilla extract.
3. Cook over medium heat, stirring occasionally, until the grapes soften and release their juices, and the mixture thickens, about 10-15 minutes.
4. Pour the grape jam filling into the prepared tart shell.
5. If using pastry dough, create a lattice or decorative top crust with strips of dough.
6. Brush the pastry crust with the egg wash.
7. Bake the tart in the preheated oven for 25-30 minutes, or until the crust is golden brown and the filling is bubbly.
8. Let the tart cool slightly before dusting with powdered sugar.
9. Serve slices of this delicious grape jam tart as a festive Easter dessert.

These holiday grape jam creations add a special touch to your seasonal celebrations, infusing classic flavors with the vibrant taste of grapes. Enjoy these delightful treats with family and friends, creating cherished memories around the holiday table.

Chapter (10) Quick and Easy Grape Jam Recipes for Busy Days

When time is of the essence, these quick and easy grape jam recipes will come to the rescue, allowing you to enjoy homemade jam without the hassle.

A. Microwave Grape Jam

Ingredients:

- 4 cups seedless grapes, washed and stemmed
- 1 cup granulated sugar
- 1 tablespoon lemon juice

Instructions:

1. Place the grapes in a microwave-safe bowl and crush them with a potato masher or fork to release their juices.
2. Stir in the sugar and lemon juice until well combined.
3. Microwave the grape mixture on high power for 5 minutes.
4. Stir the mixture and microwave for an additional 5 minutes.
5. Check the consistency of the jam—if it hasn't thickened to your desired level, microwave for another 2-3 minutes.
6. Let the jam cool for a few minutes before transferring it to sterilized jars.
7. Store the jars in the refrigerator for up to two weeks.

B. Instant Pot Grape Jam

Ingredients:

- 4 cups seedless grapes, washed and stemmed
- 1 cup granulated sugar

- 1 tablespoon lemon juice

Instructions:

1. Place the grapes, sugar, and lemon juice in the Instant Pot.
2. Close the lid and set the Instant Pot to "Manual" or "Pressure Cook" mode for 5 minutes on high pressure.
3. Once the cooking cycle is complete, allow the pressure to release naturally for 10 minutes, then perform a quick pressure release.
4. Open the lid carefully and stir the jam.
5. If the jam is not thick enough, set the Instant Pot to "Saute" mode and cook, stirring frequently, until it reaches the desired consistency.
6. Let the jam cool for a few minutes before transferring it to sterilized jars.
7. Store the jars in the refrigerator for up to two weeks.

C. One-Pot Stovetop Grape Jam
Ingredients:

- 4 cups seedless grapes, washed and stemmed
- 1 cup granulated sugar
- 1 tablespoon lemon juice

Instructions:

1. In a large saucepan, combine the grapes, sugar, and lemon juice.
2. Cook the mixture over medium heat, stirring occasionally, until the grapes break down and the mixture thickens, about 20-25 minutes.
3. Use a potato masher or fork to crush the grapes further as they cook.
4. Once the jam reaches the desired consistency, remove it from the heat and let it cool for a few minutes.

5. Transfer the jam to sterilized jars.
6. Store the jars in the refrigerator for up to two weeks.

These quick and easy grape jam recipes are perfect for busy days when you're short on time but still crave the delicious taste of homemade jam. Whether you use the microwave, Instant Pot, or stovetop, you'll have fresh grape jam ready to enjoy in no time.

Chapter (11) Artisanal Grape Jam Pairings

Elevate your culinary experience with these artisanal grape jam pairings, designed to complement and enhance a variety of flavors and textures.

A. Cheese and Grape Jam Pairing Guide

Pairing Suggestions:

1. Brie: Spread grape jam on slices of creamy Brie cheese for a delightful contrast of sweet and tangy flavors.
2. Goat Cheese: Serve grape jam alongside tangy goat cheese on crackers or crusty bread for a refreshing and flavorful combination.
3. Blue Cheese: The bold flavors of blue cheese are beautifully balanced by the sweetness of grape jam. Try this pairing on a cheese board or in a grilled cheese sandwich.
4. Manchego: Pair the nutty flavors of Manchego cheese with grape jam for a delicious Spanish-inspired treat.
5. Cheddar: The sharpness of aged Cheddar cheese is complemented by the sweetness of grape jam. Serve this pairing on crackers or apple slices for a satisfying snack.

B. Charcuterie Board with Grape Jam Accents

Ingredients:

- Assorted cured meats (such as prosciutto, salami, and chorizo)
- Variety of cheeses (such as Brie, Manchego, and blue cheese)
- Crackers and crusty bread
- Nuts (such as almonds and walnuts)
- Fresh and dried fruits (such as grapes, figs, and apricots)
- Grape jam

Assembly:

1. Arrange the cured meats and cheeses on a large serving board or platter, leaving space for accompaniments.
2. Place crackers and crusty bread in between the meats and cheeses.
3. Scatter nuts, fresh grapes, and dried fruits around the board for added texture and flavor.
4. Serve grape jam in small bowls or alongside the cheeses for dipping and spreading.
5. Encourage guests to mix and match different combinations of meats, cheeses, and grape jam for a personalized tasting experience.

C. Wine and Grape Jam Tasting Experience
Pairing Suggestions:

1. Red Wine: Pair grape jam with bold red wines such as Cabernet Sauvignon or Merlot for a rich and indulgent flavor combination.
2. White Wine: Serve grape jam with crisp white wines such as Sauvignon Blanc or Chardonnay for a refreshing and vibrant pairing.
3. Rosé: The fruity notes of rosé wine complement the sweetness of grape jam beautifully. Try this pairing for a light and summery treat.
4. Sparkling Wine: Sparkling wines such as Champagne or Prosecco are perfect for pairing with grape jam, adding a touch of elegance to any occasion.
5. Dessert Wine: Indulge in a decadent dessert pairing by serving grape jam with sweet dessert wines such as Port or Sauternes for a truly indulgent experience.

Create your own artisanal grape jam pairings by experimenting with different combinations of cheeses, charcuterie, and wines. Whether you're hosting a gathering with friends or simply enjoying a quiet evening at home, these sophisticated pairings are sure to impress your guests and tantalize your taste buds.

Chapter (12) Grape Jam Cocktails and Beverages

Infuse your favorite drinks with the rich flavors of grape jam with these delicious cocktail and beverage recipes that are perfect for any occasion.

A. Grape Jam Mojito
Ingredients:

- 2 tablespoons grape jam
- 6-8 fresh mint leaves
- 1 tablespoon lime juice
- 1 ½ ounces white rum
- Club soda
- Ice cubes
- Lime wedges and mint sprigs, for garnish

Instructions:

1. In a glass, muddle the grape jam, fresh mint leaves, and lime juice together until the mint is bruised and the jam is well incorporated.
2. Fill the glass with ice cubes.
3. Pour the white rum over the ice and stir well to combine.
4. Top off the drink with club soda.
5. Garnish with lime wedges and mint sprigs.
6. Stir gently before serving and enjoy your refreshing Grape Jam Mojito!

B. Sparkling Grape Jam Lemonade
Ingredients:

- 2 tablespoons grape jam
- 1 tablespoon fresh lemon juice
- 1 cup sparkling water or lemon-lime soda
- Ice cubes
- Lemon slices and fresh grapes, for garnish

Instructions:

1. In a glass, combine the grape jam and fresh lemon juice. Stir well until the jam is dissolved.
2. Fill the glass with ice cubes.
3. Pour the sparkling water or lemon-lime soda over the ice.
4. Stir gently to combine.
5. Garnish with lemon slices and fresh grapes.
6. Serve immediately and enjoy the refreshing taste of Sparkling Grape Jam Lemonade!

C. Grape Jam Sangria
Ingredients:

- ½ cup grape jam
- 1 bottle red wine (such as Merlot or Cabernet Sauvignon)
- ½ cup brandy
- 2 cups sparkling water or lemon-lime soda
- 1 orange, thinly sliced
- 1 lemon, thinly sliced
- 1 lime, thinly sliced
- Fresh grapes, for garnish
- Ice cubes

Instructions:

1. In a large pitcher, combine the grape jam, red wine, brandy, and sparkling water or lemon-lime soda. Stir well until the jam is

dissolved.

2. Add the sliced orange, lemon, and lime to the pitcher.
3. Chill the sangria in the refrigerator for at least 1-2 hours to allow the flavors to meld.
4. Just before serving, add ice cubes to individual glasses.
5. Pour the sangria into the glasses, making sure to include some of the fruit slices.
6. Garnish with fresh grapes.
7. Serve immediately and enjoy the fruity and refreshing flavors of Grape Jam Sangria!

These grape jam cocktails and beverages are perfect for adding a touch of sweetness and sophistication to any gathering or celebration. Whether you're sipping a Grape Jam Mojito on a hot summer day or enjoying the vibrant flavors of Grape Jam Sangria at a dinner party, these drinks are sure to impress your guests and delight your taste buds. Cheers!

Chapter (13) DIY Gifts from the Grapevine: Homemade Grape Jam Gift Ideas

Share the love of homemade grape jam with these delightful DIY gift ideas that are perfect for any occasion.

A. Grape Jam Gift Baskets

Materials Needed:

- Homemade grape jam (choose from your favorite recipe)
- Assorted crackers or breadsticks
- Selection of cheeses (such as Brie, Cheddar, and Gouda)
- Fresh fruit (such as grapes and apples)
- Nuts (such as almonds and walnuts)
- Small jars or containers for the grape jam
- Basket or decorative box
- Ribbon or twine
- Gift tags or labels

Instructions:

1. Prepare your homemade grape jam according to your favorite recipe and transfer it into small jars or containers.
2. Arrange the jars of grape jam, along with crackers, cheeses, fresh fruit, and nuts, in a basket or decorative box.
3. Use ribbon or twine to tie a bow around the basket or box.
4. Attach a gift tag or label with a personalized message, such as "Homemade Grape Jam Gift Basket - Made with Love."
5. Present the gift basket to your recipient and enjoy spreading the joy of homemade grape jam!

B. Grape Jam Mason Jar Gifts

Materials Needed:

- Homemade grape jam (choose from your favorite recipe)
- Small mason jars or jars with lids
- Fabric or decorative paper
- Ribbon or twine
- Gift tags or labels

Instructions:

1. Prepare your homemade grape jam according to your favorite recipe and transfer it into small mason jars or jars with lids.
2. Cut fabric or decorative paper into circles slightly larger than the jar lids.
3. Place the fabric or paper circles over the lids and secure them with the jar rings.
4. Tie a piece of ribbon or twine around the neck of each jar and attach a gift tag or label.
5. Optionally, add additional embellishments such as dried flowers or small ornaments.
6. Present the grape jam mason jar gifts to your recipients and watch their faces light up with joy!

C. Grape Jam Recipe Cards with Personal Touches
Materials Needed:

- Homemade grape jam (choose from your favorite recipe)
- Blank recipe cards or printable templates
- Pen or marker
- Decorative stickers or embellishments

Instructions:

1. Write down your homemade grape jam recipe on blank recipe

cards or printable templates.

2. Add personal touches to the recipe cards by including anecdotes, tips, or variations on the recipe.
3. Decorate the recipe cards with decorative stickers or embellishments to add a special touch.
4. Bundle the grape jam recipe cards together with a jar of homemade grape jam as a thoughtful gift.
5. Present the grape jam recipe cards to your recipients and share the joy of homemade cooking and gift-giving.

These DIY gift ideas allow you to share the delicious taste of homemade grape jam with your loved ones while adding a personal touch and creative flair to your presents. Whether you choose to assemble a gift basket, package grape jam in mason jars, or create personalized recipe cards, your recipients are sure to appreciate the thought and effort you put into making their gifts extra special.

Chapter (14) Farm-to-Table Grape Jam: Growing and Harvesting Your Own Grapes

Experience the joy of farm-to-table grape jam by growing and harvesting your own grapes. Follow these steps to cultivate delicious grapes in your own backyard and transform them into homemade jam.

A. Grape Varieties for Home Gardening

When selecting grape varieties for home gardening, consider factors such as climate, soil type, and intended use (fresh eating, wine making, or jam making). Here are some popular grape varieties suitable for home cultivation:

1. Concord: Known for their bold flavor and slip-skin texture, Concord grapes are excellent for making grape jam.
2. Thompson Seedless: These green grapes are sweet and juicy, perfect for fresh eating or making light-colored grape jam.
3. Muscadine: Native to the southeastern United States, muscadine grapes are well-suited to hot and humid climates. They have a unique flavor and are ideal for making jam.
4. Flame Seedless: With their vibrant red color and sweet taste, Flame Seedless grapes are great for fresh eating and making red grape jam.
5. Chardonnay: If you prefer white grape jam, consider growing Chardonnay grapes. They are versatile and can also be used for winemaking.

Choose grape varieties that thrive in your local climate and are suited to your preferences for flavor and texture.

B. Tips for Successful Grape Cultivation

Follow these tips to ensure successful grape cultivation in your home garden:

1. Choose the Right Location: Select a sunny location with well-drained soil for planting your grapevines. Ensure good air circulation to prevent diseases.
2. Plant Properly: Plant grapevines in early spring or late fall, spacing them 6-10 feet apart in rows or against a trellis or fence for support.
3. Provide Support: Install a trellis or arbor to support the grapevines as they grow. Train the vines to climb the support structure for optimal growth and fruit production.
4. Pruning: Prune grapevines annually during dormancy to remove old wood, improve air circulation, and promote fruiting.
5. Watering: Keep the soil consistently moist but not waterlogged, especially during hot and dry periods. Avoid overhead watering to prevent fungal diseases.
6. Fertilizing: Apply a balanced fertilizer in spring before new growth begins and again in early summer to support healthy growth and fruit development.
7. Pest and Disease Management: Monitor grapevines regularly for signs of pests and diseases, such as aphids, powdery mildew, and fungal infections. Use organic or chemical treatments as needed to control infestations.

C. Harvesting and Processing Grapes for Jam Making

Follow these steps to harvest and process grapes for making homemade grape jam:

1. Harvesting: Grapes are typically ready for harvest in late summer or early fall when they reach their peak ripeness. Pick grapes when they are fully colored and plump, with a slight

softness to the touch. Use pruning shears to cut clusters from the vine, leaving a small stem attached.

2. Washing: Rinse harvested grapes under cold water to remove any dirt, debris, or insects. Gently pat them dry with paper towels.

3. De-Stemming: Remove the grapes from the stems by hand or with a grape de-stemmer. Discard any unripe or damaged grapes.

4. Crushing: Crush the grapes using a potato masher, food processor, or grape crusher to release their juices.

5. Cooking: Transfer the crushed grapes to a large pot and cook them over medium heat, stirring occasionally, until they break down and release their juices.

6. Straining: Strain the cooked grapes through a fine-mesh sieve or cheesecloth to remove seeds and skins, leaving behind pure grape juice.

7. Jam Making: Follow your chosen grape jam recipe, using the strained grape juice as the main ingredient. Cook the jam according to the recipe instructions, then transfer it to sterilized jars for storage.

By following these steps for grape cultivation, harvesting, and processing, you can enjoy the satisfaction of farm-to-table grape jam made from your own homegrown grapes. Experiment with different grape varieties and jam recipes to discover your favorite flavors and techniques.

Chapter (15) Grape Jam in Savory Dishes

Explore the delightful combination of sweet and savory flavors with these creative recipes featuring grape jam as a key ingredient.

A. Grape Jam Glazed Chicken

Ingredients:

- 4 boneless, skinless chicken breasts
- Salt and pepper, to taste
- ½ cup grape jam
- 2 tablespoons soy sauce
- 2 tablespoons balsamic vinegar
- 2 cloves garlic, minced
- 1 teaspoon fresh thyme leaves
- Olive oil, for cooking
- Fresh thyme sprigs, for garnish (optional)

Instructions:

1. Season the chicken breasts with salt and pepper on both sides.
2. In a small bowl, whisk together the grape jam, soy sauce, balsamic vinegar, minced garlic, and fresh thyme leaves to make the glaze.
3. Heat a drizzle of olive oil in a large skillet over medium-high heat.
4. Add the seasoned chicken breasts to the skillet and cook for 5-6 minutes on each side, or until golden brown and cooked through.
5. Reduce the heat to medium-low and pour the grape jam glaze over the chicken breasts in the skillet.
6. Cook for an additional 2-3 minutes, stirring the glaze occasionally, until it thickens and coats the chicken evenly.

7. Remove the skillet from the heat and let the chicken rest for a few minutes.
8. Serve the grape jam glazed chicken hot, garnished with fresh thyme sprigs if desired. Enjoy the sweet and savory flavors!

B. Grape Jam Barbecue Sauce
Ingredients:

- 1 cup grape jam
- ½ cup ketchup
- 2 tablespoons apple cider vinegar
- 1 tablespoon Worcestershire sauce
- 1 teaspoon Dijon mustard
- 1 teaspoon garlic powder
- Salt and pepper, to taste

Instructions:

1. In a small saucepan, combine the grape jam, ketchup, apple cider vinegar, Worcestershire sauce, Dijon mustard, and garlic powder.
2. Stir well to combine all the ingredients.
3. Place the saucepan over medium heat and bring the mixture to a simmer.
4. Reduce the heat to low and let the barbecue sauce cook for 10-15 minutes, stirring occasionally, until it thickens to your desired consistency.
5. Season the barbecue sauce with salt and pepper to taste.
6. Remove the saucepan from the heat and let the barbecue sauce cool slightly before using it.
7. Use the grape jam barbecue sauce to baste grilled chicken, ribs, or burgers during cooking, or serve it as a dipping sauce on the side. Enjoy the tangy sweetness of this unique barbecue sauce!

C. Grape Jam Salad Dressing
Ingredients:

- ¼ cup grape jam
- 2 tablespoons balsamic vinegar
- 2 tablespoons olive oil
- 1 teaspoon Dijon mustard
- Salt and pepper, to taste

Instructions:

1. In a small bowl, whisk together the grape jam, balsamic vinegar, olive oil, and Dijon mustard until well combined.
2. Season the salad dressing with salt and pepper to taste.
3. Drizzle the grape jam salad dressing over your favorite mixed greens or salad ingredients.
4. Toss the salad gently to coat the ingredients evenly with the dressing.
5. Serve the salad immediately and enjoy the sweet and tangy flavors of the grape jam dressing!

Incorporating grape jam into savory dishes adds a unique sweetness and depth of flavor that elevates traditional recipes to new heights. Whether you're glazing chicken, making barbecue sauce, or dressing a salad, these creative recipes are sure to delight your taste buds and impress your family and friends.

Chapter (16) Grape Jam Desserts from Around the Globe

Explore the sweet and delectable world of grape jam desserts with these delightful recipes inspired by culinary traditions from France, Austria, and Greece.

A. French Grape Jam Clafoutis

Ingredients:

- 1 cup grape jam
- 3 large eggs
- 1 cup milk
- ½ cup all-purpose flour
- ¼ cup granulated sugar
- 1 teaspoon vanilla extract
- Powdered sugar, for dusting
- Fresh grapes, for garnish (optional)

Instructions:

1. Preheat your oven to 350°F (175°C). Grease a 9-inch pie dish or baking dish with butter.
2. Spread the grape jam evenly over the bottom of the prepared dish.
3. In a mixing bowl, whisk together the eggs, milk, flour, granulated sugar, and vanilla extract until smooth.
4. Pour the batter over the grape jam in the dish.
5. Bake in the preheated oven for 35-40 minutes, or until the clafoutis is puffed and golden brown on top.
6. Remove from the oven and let it cool for a few minutes.
7. Dust the clafoutis with powdered sugar before serving.
8. Garnish with fresh grapes if desired.

9. Serve warm or at room temperature. Enjoy the delightful French-inspired Grape Jam Clafoutis!

B. Austrian Grape Jam Strudel
Ingredients:

- 1 sheet of puff pastry, thawed
- 1 cup grape jam
- ½ cup breadcrumbs
- ½ cup chopped walnuts
- 2 tablespoons melted butter
- Powdered sugar, for dusting

Instructions:

1. Preheat your oven to 375°F (190°C). Line a baking sheet with parchment paper.
2. Roll out the puff pastry sheet on a lightly floured surface into a rectangle.
3. Spread the grape jam evenly over the puff pastry, leaving a border around the edges.
4. Sprinkle the breadcrumbs and chopped walnuts over the grape jam.
5. Drizzle the melted butter over the filling.
6. Roll up the puff pastry tightly, starting from one of the long sides.
7. Place the strudel seam side down on the prepared baking sheet.
8. Brush the top of the strudel with additional melted butter.
9. Bake in the preheated oven for 25-30 minutes, or until the strudel is golden brown and crispy.
10. Remove from the oven and let it cool for a few minutes before slicing.
11. Dust the strudel with powdered sugar before serving.

12. Serve warm and enjoy the delicious flavors of Austrian Grape Jam Strudel!

C. Greek Grape Jam Baklava
Ingredients:

- 1 cup grape jam
- 1 package phyllo dough, thawed
- 1 cup melted butter
- 1 cup chopped walnuts or pistachios
- 1 teaspoon ground cinnamon
- Syrup:
    - 1 cup granulated sugar
    - 1 cup water
    - 1 tablespoon lemon juice
    - 1 cinnamon stick

Instructions:

1. Preheat your oven to 350°F (175°C). Grease a baking dish with butter.
2. In a mixing bowl, combine the grape jam, chopped nuts, and ground cinnamon.
3. Place one sheet of phyllo dough in the prepared baking dish and brush it with melted butter.
4. Repeat layering phyllo sheets and brushing each layer with butter until you have used half of the phyllo sheets.
5. Spread the grape jam and nut mixture evenly over the layered phyllo sheets.
6. Continue layering the remaining phyllo sheets on top, brushing each layer with butter.
7. Using a sharp knife, carefully cut the baklava into diamond or square shapes.

8. Bake in the preheated oven for 45-50 minutes, or until the baklava is golden brown and crisp.
9. While the baklava is baking, prepare the syrup. In a saucepan, combine the sugar, water, lemon juice, and cinnamon stick. Bring to a boil, then reduce the heat and simmer for 10-15 minutes, until slightly thickened.
10. Remove the baklava from the oven and immediately pour the hot syrup over the hot baklava.
11. Let the baklava cool completely in the pan before serving.
12. Serve at room temperature and enjoy the delightful Greek-inspired Grape Jam Baklava!

Indulge in the sweet and exotic flavors of these grape jam desserts from around the globe, each offering a unique and delicious taste experience. Whether you're savoring the French-inspired Clafoutis, the Austrian-style Strudel, or the Greek delicacy Baklava, these desserts are sure to impress and delight your taste buds.

Chapter (17) The Art of Pairing Wine with Grape Jam

Discover the delightful synergy of wine and grape jam with these tips and ideas for pairing these two complementary flavors.

A. Wine and Grape Jam Pairing Basics

Pairing wine with grape jam involves finding complementary flavors and balancing sweetness levels. Here are some basic guidelines to help you create harmonious wine and grape jam pairings:

1. Consider Wine Varieties: Choose wines that complement the flavor profile of the grape jam. For example, a sweet jam might pair well with a dessert wine, while a tangy jam could be balanced by a crisp white wine.

2. Match Sweetness Levels: Balance the sweetness of the jam with the sweetness of the wine. Sweeter jams pair best with sweeter wines, while tart jams can be paired with drier wines to create contrast.

3. Think about Intensity: Consider the intensity of flavors in both the wine and the jam. Lighter jams may pair well with lighter-bodied wines, while richer, more robust jams can stand up to fuller-bodied wines.

4. Experiment: Don't be afraid to experiment with different wine and grape jam pairings to discover your favorite combinations. Taste test small amounts of jam with different wines to find the perfect match.

B. Wine Tasting Events featuring Grape Jam

Host wine tasting events featuring grape jam to explore the diverse world of wine and jam pairings with friends and family. Here's how to organize a successful tasting event:

1. Select a Variety of Wines: Choose a selection of wines ranging from sparkling and white to red and dessert wines. Consider including wines with different flavor profiles and sweetness levels to accommodate various preferences.

2. Prepare Grape Jam Pairings: Pair each wine with a complementary grape jam, taking into account the wine's characteristics and flavor profile. Provide small tasting spoons or crackers for guests to sample the jams alongside the wines.

3. Provide Tasting Notes: Create tasting notes or guides that describe each wine and its suggested grape jam pairing. Include information about flavor profiles, sweetness levels, and tasting tips to help guests appreciate the nuances of each pairing.

4. Encourage Exploration: Encourage guests to explore the wine and jam pairings at their own pace, discussing their impressions and preferences with each other. Provide opportunities for guests to share their tasting experiences and insights.

5. Offer Food Pairings: Enhance the tasting experience by offering food pairings that complement the wines and grape jams. Consider serving cheese, charcuterie, fresh fruit, and other snacks that enhance the flavors of the wine and jam combinations.

C. Hosting a Wine and Grape Jam Soiree

Invite friends and family to a wine and grape jam soiree where they can enjoy a variety of wine and jam pairings in a festive atmosphere. Here's how to host a memorable event:

1. Set the Scene: Create an inviting atmosphere with cozy lighting, comfortable seating, and elegant table decorations. Consider using wine-themed decor such as wine barrels, corks, and grapevine wreaths to set the mood.

2. Offer a Selection of Wines: Provide a diverse selection of wines for guests to sample, including sparkling, white, red, and dessert

wines. Chill white and sparkling wines beforehand and offer red wines at the appropriate temperature.

3. Display Grape Jam Pairings: Set up a tasting station where guests can sample different grape jams paired with each wine. Label each jam with the corresponding wine and provide tasting notes to guide guests through the experience.

4. Provide Wine Education: Offer brief wine education sessions or guided tastings led by a knowledgeable host or sommelier. Share information about wine varieties, flavor profiles, and pairing tips to enhance guests' understanding and appreciation of the wines.

5. Encourage Socializing: Create opportunities for guests to mingle, socialize, and share their tasting experiences with each other. Consider incorporating interactive elements such as wine-themed games or trivia to keep guests engaged and entertained.

By exploring the art of pairing wine with grape jam, you can create memorable tasting experiences that tantalize the senses and foster a deeper appreciation for both wine and jam. Whether hosting a wine tasting event or a casual soiree, these tips and ideas will help you create a delightful and enjoyable experience for all your guests. Cheers to the perfect wine and jam pairing!

Chapter (18) Preserving Grape Jam Traditions: Family Recipes and Stories

Discover the rich heritage of grape jam traditions with these heartwarming tales and cherished recipes passed down through generations.

A. Passing Down Generational Grape Jam Recipes

Family recipes for grape jam are treasured heirlooms that connect generations and evoke fond memories of home. Here's how families continue to pass down these beloved recipes:

1. Recipe Sharing: Families gather together to share their cherished grape jam recipes, often handwritten on weathered recipe cards or passed down orally from one generation to the next.

2. Teaching and Learning: Elders impart their knowledge and expertise in jam making to younger family members, teaching them the art of selecting the finest grapes, cooking the jam to perfection, and preserving it for future enjoyment.

3. Adapting to Modern Times: While preserving the essence of traditional grape jam recipes, families also embrace modern techniques and ingredients to suit contemporary tastes and lifestyles.

4. Creating New Memories: Making grape jam becomes a beloved family tradition, with each generation adding their own unique twist to the recipes and creating new memories together in the kitchen.

B. Memories of Grape Jam Making

Grape jam making is more than just a culinary activity—it's a bonding experience that brings families together and creates lasting memories. Here are some cherished memories of grape jam making:

1. Harvesting Together: Families gather in vineyards or backyard gardens to harvest ripe grapes, working side by side to fill baskets with plump, juicy fruit.
2. Kitchen Stories: The kitchen becomes the heart of the home as families come together to wash, de-stem, and cook the grapes, sharing stories, laughter, and occasional mishaps along the way.
3. Aromas and Flavors: The sweet aroma of cooking grape jam fills the air, transporting family members back to their childhoods and evoking memories of past jam-making sessions.
4. Tasting and Sampling: As the jam cooks, family members eagerly sample spoonfuls of the warm, sticky mixture, savoring the flavors and offering feedback on sweetness levels and texture.
5. Preserving Tradition: Once the jam is ready, families work together to fill jars, label them with care, and preserve them for future enjoyment, ensuring that the tradition of grape jam making lives on for generations to come.

C. Celebrating Grape Jam as a Cultural Tradition

Grape jam holds a special place in many cultures around the world, celebrated for its delicious flavor and cultural significance. Here's how families honor grape jam as a cherished tradition:

1. Festival Celebrations: In some regions, grape harvest festivals are held to celebrate the bounty of the season, with grape jam making demonstrations, tastings, and competitions.
2. Culinary Heritage: Grape jam recipes are passed down from one generation to the next, preserving culinary heritage and cultural identity for future generations to enjoy.

3. Community Gatherings: Families and neighbors come together for community jam-making events, sharing resources, knowledge, and camaraderie as they work together to produce delicious homemade jam.
4. Artisanal Craftsmanship: Some families take pride in the artisanal craftsmanship of their homemade grape jam, using traditional methods and locally sourced ingredients to create a product that reflects their cultural heritage and values.
5. Sharing and Generosity: Grape jam is often shared as a symbol of hospitality and generosity, with families offering jars of homemade jam to friends, neighbors, and guests as tokens of appreciation and goodwill.

By preserving grape jam traditions through the sharing of family recipes, the creation of lasting memories, and the celebration of cultural heritage, families ensure that the art of jam making continues to thrive for generations to come.

Chapter (19) Grape Jam Adventures: Culinary Tourism and Grape Harvest Festivals

Embark on a culinary journey celebrating the beloved grape jam with these exciting adventures in culinary tourism and grape harvest festivals.

A. Visiting Grape Jam Producers Around the World

Experience the magic of grape jam production firsthand by visiting grape jam producers around the world. Here's how to plan your grape jam culinary tour:

1. Research Grape Jam Producers: Start by researching grape jam producers in regions known for their grape cultivation and jam-making traditions. Look for family-owned farms, artisanal producers, and specialty shops that offer tours and tastings.

2. Plan Your Itinerary: Create an itinerary that includes visits to multiple grape jam producers in different locations. Consider exploring diverse grape varieties, production methods, and flavor profiles to gain a deeper understanding of the art of grape jam making.

3. Take Guided Tours: Take guided tours of grape jam production facilities to learn about the entire process, from grape harvesting and processing to cooking and packaging. Ask questions, interact with producers, and sample a variety of grape jams along the way.

4. Attend Tastings and Workshops: Attend tastings and workshops led by grape jam experts to explore different flavor combinations, learn about regional culinary traditions, and discover new techniques for enjoying grape jam in cooking and baking.

5. Shop for Souvenirs: Browse onsite shops and markets to

purchase your favorite grape jams, as well as other local products and gourmet goodies to bring home as souvenirs or gifts for friends and family.

B. Participating in Grape Harvest Festivals

Immerse yourself in the vibrant atmosphere of grape harvest festivals, where you can celebrate the bounty of the season and indulge in all things grape-related. Here's how to make the most of your grape harvest festival experience:

1. Find Festivals Near You: Research grape harvest festivals in your area or travel to renowned grape-growing regions known for their festive celebrations. Check local event listings, tourism websites, and social media for upcoming festivals and events.
2. Enjoy Grape-themed Activities: Attend grape-themed activities and events such as grape stomping competitions, vineyard tours, wine tastings, and cooking demonstrations featuring grape jam and other grape-based delicacies.
3. Sample Local Cuisine: Indulge in delicious dishes made with fresh grapes and grape products, including grape jam, wine, juice, and preserves. Explore food stalls, farmers' markets, and local restaurants to taste the flavors of the season.
4. Experience Cultural Performances: Enjoy live music, dance performances, and cultural celebrations that showcase the rich heritage and traditions of grape-growing regions around the world.
5. Connect with the Community: Engage with local farmers, producers, and artisans to learn about their craft, exchange stories, and forge lasting connections with the community. Embrace the spirit of hospitality and camaraderie that defines grape harvest festivals.

C. Cooking Classes and Workshops focused on Grape Jam

Enhance your culinary skills and deepen your appreciation for grape jam with hands-on cooking classes and workshops led by expert chefs and jam makers. Here's how to get involved:

1. Find Cooking Classes: Look for cooking schools, culinary institutes, and community centers that offer classes and workshops focused on grape jam making and cooking. Check online listings, event calendars, and local publications for upcoming opportunities.

2. Learn New Techniques: Join cooking classes led by experienced instructors who will teach you essential techniques for making grape jam from scratch, as well as creative recipes for incorporating grape jam into a variety of dishes.

3. Experiment with Flavors: Explore different grape varieties, flavor combinations, and culinary applications of grape jam in cooking and baking. Get hands-on experience experimenting with ingredients and developing your own unique recipes.

4. Connect with Fellow Food Enthusiasts: Connect with like-minded food enthusiasts and fellow grape jam aficionados in a supportive and collaborative learning environment. Share tips, swap recipes, and build friendships with fellow participants.

5. Take Home Delicious Creations: Enjoy the satisfaction of creating delicious grape jam and culinary creations from scratch during your cooking classes and workshops. Take home your homemade jams, baked goods, and newfound culinary skills to share with family and friends.

By embarking on grape jam adventures through culinary tourism, grape harvest festivals, and cooking classes, you'll gain a deeper appreciation for the art of grape jam making and the rich cultural heritage of grape-growing regions around the world. Let your taste buds guide you on a flavorful journey of discovery and delight!

Chapter (20) The Future of Grape Jam: Innovations and Trends

Explore the exciting future of grape jam with emerging flavors, sustainable practices, and advancements in food technology and innovation.

A. Emerging Grape Jam Flavors and Varieties

As consumer tastes evolve and culinary trends shift, grape jam producers are experimenting with new flavors and varieties to meet the demands of modern palates. Here are some emerging trends to watch for:

1. Exotic Fruit Combinations: Expect to see grape jams infused with exotic fruits such as mango, passion fruit, and lychee, creating unique flavor profiles that tantalize the taste buds.

2. Herbal and Floral Infusions: Look for grape jams enhanced with herbal and floral infusions such as lavender, rosemary, and elderflower, adding complexity and sophistication to traditional recipes.

3. Spiced and Seasoned Varieties: Explore grape jams featuring bold spices and seasonings such as cinnamon, cardamom, and ginger, inspired by global culinary traditions and fusion cuisine.

4. Limited Edition Releases: Keep an eye out for limited edition grape jams made with rare grape varieties or seasonal ingredients, offering exclusive flavor experiences for discerning consumers.

5. Health-Focused Formulations: With growing interest in health and wellness, expect to see grape jams formulated with functional ingredients such as superfoods, probiotics, and adaptogens to support overall well-being.

B. Sustainable Practices in Grape Jam Production

In response to environmental concerns and consumer demand for ethically sourced products, grape jam producers are embracing sustainable practices throughout the production process. Here's how sustainability is shaping the future of grape jam production:

1. Organic and Non-GMO Ingredients: More grape jam producers are sourcing organic and non-GMO grapes to minimize pesticide use and promote soil health, ensuring a cleaner and more sustainable product.

2. Reduced Packaging Waste: Companies are exploring innovative packaging solutions such as recyclable jars, compostable labels, and eco-friendly shipping materials to reduce packaging waste and minimize environmental impact.

3. Energy-Efficient Production Methods: Grape jam manufacturers are investing in energy-efficient equipment and production methods to reduce carbon emissions and conserve natural resources during manufacturing processes.

4. Supporting Local Farmers: Many grape jam producers are partnering with local farmers and vineyards to source grapes locally, supporting small-scale agriculture and reducing transportation-related emissions.

5. Water Conservation Measures: In regions prone to water scarcity, grape jam producers are implementing water-saving techniques such as drip irrigation, rainwater harvesting, and water recycling to minimize water usage and promote sustainability.

C. Grape Jam in the Age of Food Technology and Innovation

Advancements in food technology and innovation are revolutionizing the way grape jam is produced, packaged, and consumed. Here are some exciting developments to watch for in the future:

1. Smart Packaging Solutions: Explore smart packaging solutions

equipped with sensors and RFID technology that provide real-time information about product freshness, shelf life, and storage conditions to ensure optimal quality and safety.

2. Plant-Based Alternatives: With the rise of plant-based diets, expect to see more plant-based alternatives to traditional grape jam made from innovative ingredients such as fruit pectin, agar agar, and konjac root, catering to vegan and vegetarian consumers.

3. Customizable Flavor Profiles: Discover customizable grape jam formulations that allow consumers to personalize their jam preferences by adjusting sweetness levels, fruit concentrations, and flavor intensities to suit individual tastes and dietary preferences.

4. Augmented Reality Experiences: Engage with grape jam brands through immersive augmented reality experiences that offer interactive storytelling, virtual tastings, and educational content to enhance consumer engagement and brand loyalty.

5. Blockchain Traceability: Trace the journey of your grape jam from farm to table with blockchain technology, providing transparent and verifiable information about sourcing, production, and distribution practices to build trust and transparency in the supply chain.

By embracing emerging flavors, sustainable practices, and technological innovations, the future of grape jam is poised to be deliciously diverse, environmentally friendly, and technologically advanced. Get ready to embark on a flavorful journey of discovery and innovation as grape jam continues to evolve in the years to come.

❖ Conclusion

As we wrap up our exploration of grape jam and its culinary journey, let's reflect on some final thoughts and tips for perfecting your grape jam-making adventures.

A. Final Tips and Tricks for Perfect Grape Jam

1. Choose Ripe Grapes: Opt for ripe, flavorful grapes when making grape jam to ensure the best taste and texture.
2. Balance Sweetness: Adjust the amount of sugar in your jam recipe to achieve the perfect balance of sweetness, depending on the natural sweetness of the grapes and your personal preference.
3. Add Citrus for Brightness: Enhance the flavor of your grape jam by adding a splash of lemon juice or zest for a bright, citrusy note.
4. Use Pectin for Set: If your grapes are low in natural pectin, consider adding commercial pectin to help your jam set properly and achieve the desired consistency.
5. Sterilize Jars Properly: Ensure your jars are sterilized and properly sealed to prolong the shelf life of your grape jam and prevent spoilage.

B. Encouragement to Explore Further Jam-Making Adventures

Embarking on the journey of making grape jam opens up a world of culinary creativity and exploration. Don't be afraid to experiment with different grape varieties, flavor combinations, and cooking techniques to create unique and delicious jams that reflect your tastes and preferences.

Explore further jam-making adventures by trying out new recipes, attending cooking classes, and connecting with fellow jam enthusiasts. Share your creations with friends and family, and embrace the joy of homemade preserves that bring people together and evoke memories of warmth and comfort.

C. Closing Thoughts on the Versatility and Joy of Grape Jam

Grape jam is more than just a sweet spread—it's a symbol o tradition, creativity, and culinary craftsmanship. Its versatility allows i to be enjoyed in a variety of ways, from simple toast to gourmet dishes desserts, and beverages.

As you savor the flavors of grape jam, remember the joy it brings t your palate and the memories it creates with each spoonful. Whethe you're indulging in classic grape jam recipes or exploring innovativ flavor combinations, let the versatility and joy of grape jam continue t inspire your culinary adventures for years to come.

9 798224 441310